BROKEN TO BRILLIANT

PRAISE FOR BROKEN TO BRILLIANT

"When you pick up this book, cancel all other plans because you won't be able to put it down until you're done! This is a magnificent story of triumph over adversity that will inspire you to know miracles abound, and that YOU have the power to choose what you believe and experience in YOUR life."

— BEV ADAMO OWNER/CEO–WILD & WISE®
ENTERPRISES

"Part inspiration, part personal development, part stories that leave you at the edge of your seat, *Broken to Brilliant* is full of practical ways to connect the dots of your life and know that 'Anything is possible.'"

— ADAM MARKEL, #1 WSJ BESTSELLING
AUTHOR OF PIVOT

"In this often crazy and unpredictable world, to find a person who has faced struggle and refused to play "victim" is refreshing. Witnessing Gary overcome and utilize his trauma, strife and struggle to become the very best version of himself, is awe-inspiring and humbling. While I read, I kept returning to this sentence early in the book '...*lack of awareness of our unconscious beliefs is what is holding us back from following our dreams, creating the life we desire, or reaching our full potential.*' For anyone looking for a wise and powerful story full of inspiration, this book is a must."

> — KASEY MATHEWS, SPEAKER, COACH AND
> AUTHOR OF PREEMIE: LESSONS IN LOVE,
> LIFE AND MOTHERHOOD AND A MOM'S
> GUIDE TO CREATING A MAGICAL LIFE

"Gary's personal story is inspirational and transformational. This powerful book showed me how having a new perspective makes all the difference in the world. I now believe and know 'Anything is possible.'"

> — MARCIA WIEDER, CEO, DREAM
> UNIVERSITY AND BEST SELLING AUTHOR

BROKEN TO

Overcome Obstacles to Create
Opportunities and Achieve the Impossible

BRILLIANT

GARY BUCKMANN

Very
Grateful
Publishing

To my loving wife, Victoria. I dedicate this book to her for countless reasons, the least of which is her love for me. She taught me how the universe works and there is abundance in this world, and there is more than enough for everyone. Without her guidance, inspiration, motivation, and constant support, I would have never, ever, in my life taken on such a project. It is a miracle I am an author of a book, because all my life everyone convinced me I had terrible writing skills. Victoria convinced me otherwise, and you are reading the proof right now. I thank God every day for bringing her into my life. Victoria, I love you and thank you with all my being!

CONTENTS

"Awareness is like the sun. When it shines on things, they are transformed."

— *NHAT HANH*

PREFACE

My coaching career started in 1968 and officially ended in 2014. During my forty-six-year career as a coach, I was fortunate enough to reach the highest level in my sport. Only a handful of coaches ever become a USA National Team coach in any sport. Not only did I get to travel the world with the USA Team and work with Olympians, I coached a gymnast from our gym onto the USA team every year of my elite competitive experience, which spanned over an eight-year period. I helped develop multiple state and regional championship teams, including the last official private club national championship team in 1977. I also coached numerous individual athletes to state, regional, and national championship status. I'm proud to say that almost all of my national competitors received full ride scholarships to major universities across the United States.

I became a USA National Team Coach and the head coach of the USA Junior Elite National Team. I took Olympic gold medal winner Marylou Retton on her very first international trip, and traveled to Japan with Peter Vidmar, Tim Daggett, and Mitch Gaylord, all 1984 Olympic gold medal winners. I taught Brian Boitano, the 1988 men's singles ice-skating Olympic gold medal winner, a back flip. And I was the master clinician at national symposiums in the United States, Canada, New Zealand, and South Africa. I don't say this to boast about my coaching career. I'm telling you all this because if anyone would have told me that I would accomplish this when I was lying flat on my back, paralyzed in a hospital bed, I would have laughed in their face and said, "No freaking way!"

All of this was possible thanks to many factors and many people, but it required me to take an arduous journey.

My transformational awareness journey began at age twenty when I broke my neck and was paralyzed. My accident caused me to look at my life from a whole new perspective. Writing this book allowed me to develop a new awareness on why my life unfolded the way it did. More importantly, it exposed the truth of what really happened, instead of the stories I told myself to feel safe and make sense of my life. All of our experiences and life stories have shaped us. How we interpreted and gave meaning to those stories formed the beliefs of who we think we are and what we're capable of. This is the exact awareness I wanted to expose. Often, we believe that things in life, like this horrendous accident of mine, happened *to* us. I now believe life happens *for* us.

What if you could gain a new awareness, a new perspective of your experiences and begin to uncover the potential gift in each one of them. This new perspective might give you a whole new outlook on why *everything happens for a reason.*

I took all the information I acquired and the teachings I benefited from, added all of my own experiences, and I adapted it to create a program of my own. I have always thought that learning a skill or achieving a goal in sports is no different than learning a skill or achieving a goal in life.

The exact same mindset, discipline, dedication, and step by step procedures are required.

It might sound crazy, but I've always said breaking my neck was one of the best things that ever happened to me. I truly believe that injury forced me to look at things differently and depend on my own inner-knowing. It caused a compound effect, enabling me to create an amazing life that I could never have imagined.

What if many of the 'so called' bad things that happened to you in your life, are actually the catalysts that created all the good things in your life? What if there is no good or bad? What if all of our perceptions of who we think we are and what we're capable of doing, are just skewed perceptions of our own minds? Do you think that discovering the real truth by connecting the dots of your life would be something you'd like to be aware of? I hope so.

While writing this book, I had quite a few aha moments. When I started the book, I had no idea where it would lead me. Reviewing all of my stories from childhood into adulthood, a new awareness of the truth was revealed. In hindsight, I was able to identify all the gifts that actually occurred from all my experiences rather than the stories I told myself. I exposed beliefs, resulting from experiences that defined me for decades, and it gave me a new truth of why they really happened. For the first time in my life, self-perceptions that held me back from reaching my full potential hit me like a bucket of cold water being thrown in my face. Additionally, I uncovered core beliefs that inspired me to go beyond what I thought was possible. All the little things I learned from childhood through adolescence made a huge difference in accomplishing the so-called impossible.

Through it all, I realized that the truth, not my interpretation of the truth, is what I needed to become aware of in order to make sense of my life and be happy. My intention for sharing my stories and connecting the dots of my life is to spark awareness of memories in your life. When looked at from a new perspective, it might connect the dots for you, giving you an opportunity to have some powerful eye-opening experiences of your own and allow you to transform your past and more importantly your future. I invite you to take a look at your life from a whole new point of view. To see how some experiences that you may have labeled as 'bad' ultimately turned out to be the gifts that led to the amazing experiences that occurred in your life.

Lack of awareness is what caused my accident.

Lack of awareness of our unconscious beliefs is what is holding us back from following our dreams, creating the life we desire, or reaching our full potential in any area of our lives.

We all have the capacity to create the impossible in our lives, simply by becoming aware and gaining a new perspective of why things happened the way they did. By looking at the experiences in your life and connecting the dots for yourself to reveal the truth of what really happened, instead of your perception of what happened your life will be transformed. This new found awareness will allow you to do the so called impossible.

Anything is possible. I'm living proof of that fact. If I can do it so can you!

1

THE VAULT

I stood at the end of a sixty-five-foot-long rubber runway. I began to slow down my breathing, aligning my breath with my focus–a practice I've been mastering for years. The vaulting horse waited erect at the end of the runway, daring me once again to attempt the same vault I'd already attempted ten times. Each and every time so far, I was left sprawled out on the landing mat, staring up at the horse; a rider once again thrown. But I wasn't raised to quit, ever. I stared down at the horse, assuring it I would persevere no matter what it took.

Looking back, I imagine the horse laughing at my ignorance, because I had no idea the price I would pay.

I paused, visualizing all the different components of this multiple flipping vault, trying to overcome my frustration. Internally, I doubted whether or not I should even attempt such an advanced, complex vault. I repeated my mental preparation, inhaled deeply, and took off down the runway. With each step, I gained more speed. Just before my feet hit the carpeted springboard that would propel me onto and over the horse, I felt my right foot step down on the runway. Instantly, I knew I'd made a mistake. I was in big trouble. I'd taken off on the wrong foot.

As my hands made contact with the horse, everything moved in slow motion. In a split second that felt like minutes, my mind threw questions at me that I didn't have the answers for. Not knowing where I was in the air or how much power I had just generated, I asked myself, "Do I kick out to a simple handspring without the front flip and save myself?" I heard my inner voice egging me on, "Hey Gary, go for it!"

But I didn't want to crash and burn again. I was tired of smashing into the four-inch unforgiving landing mat on the hardwood floor. I regretted the decision to remove the crash pad. The twelve-inch foam buffer between me and the landing mat. Pushing off my arms and opening my shoulder angle to initiate the vault, I made a snap decision mid-air to kick out. Thinking it was the right decision to save my body from another crash landing.

I had no idea that I had created way too much height and rotation. Because I had skipped steps in my training, I had zero awareness of where I was in the air. The next thing I knew, I was aimed headfirst about a foot and a half from the floor, like an arrow being shot into the ground. There wasn't even enough time to get my hands out in front of me to save myself. In a one-second eternity, all these thoughts tumbled through my mind just before my head hit with a shattering thud.

I woke up dazed and confused lying flat on my back, not knowing how much time had passed since I got knocked out. A tight net circle of shocked silent faces leaned over me. My coach and all my teammates, eyes glaring and mouths gaping, stared down at me in horror.

Totally disoriented and not quite sure what had just

happened, I felt the need to speak up and assure them I was ok. I said nothing. I wanted to reach out and have them pull me back up, slap me on the back, and tell me that I'd get it the next time. But I was pretty certain there'd never be a next time. I couldn't feel anything from my neck down.

2

CAR JUMP

I t was a bright sunny day in Martinez, California. Mom loaded my one-year old baby sister, Carol, and me into our four-door white Chevy sedan to go grocery shopping. Mom strapped Carol in a baby seat up front with her, but as a three-year-old, I got to ride in the backseat by myself.

Mom backed the car out of the garage and stopped in the driveway to get out and close the garage door. It was 1954, long before the days of automatic garage door openers. Our car was a stick shift, so she put the car in neutral and got out. I watched my tiny mom pull on the rope to close the big solid wood heavy garage door. As I watched her, I felt the car start to roll. Instantly my body stiffened up and my heart pounded as I realized the car was moving backwards down the driveway. I called out to my mother while pounding my little fists on the backseat window. Facing the garage door with her back to us, she couldn't hear my screams. Without another thought, I pulled the door handle down, kicked the back door open, stood up on the edge of the seat, and broad jumped out of the car onto the lawn. Simultaneously, my mother turned around just in time to see me jump and the car rolling

4

backwards. I stood in awe, never knowing my mom was capable of running so fast. She flung the car door open and jumped inside. I watched as her tiny arm reached under the dashboard and pull the handle of the emergency brake. She stopped the car before it reached the busy street in front of our house.

All the while, I stood on the lawn chin up, chest puffed out, feeling like superman who just saved the day. I was tingling all over from the adrenaline pumping through my entire body from jumping out of the car and living to talk about it. I was so proud of myself for reacting so fast. I had followed my gut instinct and saved my own life. In the next moment, I saw my mother jumping out of the car walking briskly towards me. I imagined the pride she must be feeling at her son's quick thinking. In my mind's eye I saw her hugging me, kissing me, and congratulating me for being so brave.

Boy was I wrong! Instead she grabbed me by the arm and started smacking my behind, yelling and screaming at the top of her lungs. "You could have been killed! Never ever jump out of a moving car. What were you thinking? Your little sister didn't jump out of the car!"

My first thought was, "Great, I just saved my own life, only to have my mother beat me within an inch of it." My three-year-old mind was spinning out of control, totally confused. Sitting in the backseat of a backwards rolling car, with no one behind the wheel, led to death! This is where my mind started filling in the blanks. Hurt, confused, filled with shame, and totally disappointed, I created my own truth about what just happened. This cocktail of emotions, from being proud of myself to fuming with anger and blanketed with sadness, caused me to make up a story that made sense of it all.

Our minds make up stories in order to make sense out of

things, without us even being aware of it. My new truth became, "It's painful to follow my instincts. It's a bad thing, and if I do, I'll get punished for it." In that moment a new belief was formed that dictated my future actions.

We all have this innate wisdom that we are born with. Whether you call it intuition, gut instinct or following a hunch, it's there to guide us in our lives. Yet, for most of us, it is beaten out of us in childhood, in my case literally.

The day of my accident, I had a gut feeling that I should have stopped vaulting after the tenth vault while I was still ahead. But that same cocktail of emotions took over, and I ignored my inner voice. That day, I didn't follow my gut, and it cost me dearly.

3

RACING MOM

My mother was four foot eleven inches tall and weighed a mere ninety-five pounds soaking wet. Standing next to my dad, who stood at nearly six feet, she looked tiny. Even though I was small at five years old, I was already shoulder height to my mother. Despite her small stature, I was very afraid of her. Maybe afraid isn't quite the correct term. I guess I'd say I had total respect for her. A strong Iowa farm girl, she carried herself with confidence and didn't tolerate any nonsense. She was powerful even at her size. She constantly reminded me that dynamite came in small packages. She made me believe I could do anything when I put my heart and mind into it. She was quick, clever, and had her own subtle ways of getting her point across to us kids. For example: I learned a great lesson about humility and goal setting from her in our own backyard one day.

I don't remember how the challenge came about, but I'm sure it was my five-year-old ego and my big mouth that started it all. I decided to let my Mom know that I could run faster than her, and no matter what, she would never be able to catch me. It was a hot summer day when we were out in the yard working, and I threw out the challenge. Mom grinned back at me, nodded her head, and in her quiet but firm voice, told me "Go ahead, take off, let's see if you can outrun me."

We had a spacious backyard with a long stretch of grass, perfect for a sprint race. I crouched down, pushed off my back foot, and took off. I was sure I'd leave my mom in the dust, but when I looked back over my shoulder, there she was right on top of me. My arms pumped back and forth as fast as they could go; my thighs were burning. I was running at full throttle, but I couldn't shake her. I kept looking back and jeering, "You'll never catch me!"

She replied, "You'd better look where you are going."

Of course, being of the male persuasion, I didn't listen. Before I could throw out another smart ass remark my mom came to a screeching halt without saying a word. I turned back to see where I was going and immediately smacked chin first into our very hard, six-foot redwood fence. Before I knew what happened, I was all the way through the fence and flat on my back in our neighbor's grassy yard. As I reached up to feel my red-hot burning chin from the newly acquired Redwood splinters, I realized that my loving mother let me run full speed right into the fence! She stepped over the boards that I had knocked down with my face into the neighbor's yard. Towering over me, looking me square in the eyes, nodding her head she quietly agreed, "I guess you're right. You can outrun me."

Years later, looking through old yearbooks, I discovered that my mother was a track star. She was on the relay team when she was in high school. What I didn't know then, but that I know so well today, is my mother hadn't run her fastest that day in the backyard. She ran just fast enough to teach me an important lesson in humility and a valuable lesson in goal setting that served me well as an athlete and a coach. Mom planted a seed that day that has stuck with me; keep your eye on your goals and keep looking forward in order to know where you're going. A philosophy that was imperative later when faced with paralysis from a broken neck.

4

TOY STORY

When I was six years old, I had to go into the hospital for a hernia operation. Back in the fifties, you knew all your neighbors, and everyone was like family. Being the first kid on our block to be hospitalized, everyone came to see me, bearing gifts. There were at least thirty houses on our block, so by the time I got out of the hospital, I had boxes full of toys, even a new Raleigh first baseman's baseball glove! I had so many new toys my mother sewed me a humongous white terry cloth bag with my name on it in big red letters to hold them all.

Early one morning, I pulled my huge bag out of the closet and dumped all my new toys onto my bedroom floor. It was a little boy's dream–wall to wall toys. I sat on my bedroom floor, picking up the new model truck, train, and soldiers, playing with each and every one of those toys for hours. Several times that morning, Mom swung the door open and stuck her head in to remind me to put all my toys back where they belonged when I was done. Each time she poked her head in, I just picked up a new toy, continued playing, and ignored her. My lack of response and nonchalant attitude must have triggered something in her, because the third time she poked her head in the doorway, she gave me an ultimatum. "If you don't put all your toys away," shaking her finger at me, "I'm going to throw them in the garbage can."

I smirked and shook my head in disbelief, knowing darn well that she'd never throw away brand new toys. When I'd had enough of my new toys, I got up and ran outside to play with my friends, totally dismissing her warning.

After playing for an hour or so I came back into the house. I trotted into my room and all my toys were gone! I immediately ran to the kitchen, screaming, "Where are all my toys?"

Without turning around from the kitchen sink, my mother replied, "They're in the garbage can."

I gasped, feeling like I had just been punched in the stomach. Red faced and crying out of control, I pleaded with and begged her to let me have my toys back.

"I told you what would happen if you didn't put your toys away," she said, wiping her hands on a dish towel.

I bolted out the back door to rescue my toys. She ran right behind me and grabbed me by the arm, pulling me away from the garbage can. I was upset and pleading through the tears streaming down my face; my mother remained stoic. It was like it didn't even phase her. She gave me a quick spank and sent me to my room. The next morning, the garbage man arrived. Standing motionless at the living room window, I watched as he emptied all the trash, including my toys, into the big dirty blue truck.

To this day, I remember the helpless feeling of standing at the window and watching all my toys disappear. As hard as it was, I now realize my mother had modeled the power of making a decision and keeping your word, not only to someone else, but more importantly, keeping your word and integrity with yourself. This quality mom modeled that very sad day was the imperative step that helped me years later when I was in the hospital. I made a decision to not accept the diagnosis the doctors gave me and heal myself. I'm happy to report that I kept my word even when I had no idea how I was going to pull it off.

This same skill allowed me to become a very successful coach. During my coaching career when I said this is the way it is, I never wavered, so everyone knew exactly where they stood with me and that it was non-negotiable.

5

DAD

I learned a lot of lessons from Dad too. My dad was intelligent, funny, multi-talented and a perfectionist. It seemed to me that there wasn't anything he couldn't do. He was well versed in mechanics, carpentry, bricklaying, landscaping, and cement work; you name it he did it. He even drew up the blueprints for the additional room we added on to our house. I have no idea where he learned all these different skills because my grandfather was a doctor. I wish I had asked.

My entire childhood and throughout my high school years, my dad included me in projects around the house and taught me how to do practical work. My first memory was the year before I started kindergarten when I got to operate the rotor-tiller with him at our new house in Sacramento. We had to prepare the ground to plant the lawn and flower beds my parents wanted to have in both the front and back yards. He put my small body in front of his, and I felt his strong arms on top of mine. He showed me the handle to engage the blades and the power handle to make the blades rotate, and together we tilled the ground. He taught me how to run a lawn mower and how to mow lawns. How to use a hammer, a hand saw, a skill saw, table saw, and a drill for building shelves, cabinets, and furniture. He showed me how to use every tool in his toolbox to fix and repair things. "These are skills you will need in life," he repeatedly said while we worked side by side. I learned how to paint by hand and to spray paint, how to build a coaster race cart, how to repair and fix my bikes, toys, and cars. Hell, I even learned how to frame and build an extra room on our house.

Time spent with my dad learning and developing all these skills was wonderful, yet in my mind there was a drawback. It wasn't what I was learning, but how Dad was teaching me–the method he used. He never told me I was doing anything wrong, but his actions spoke louder to me than his words. He didn't have the patience to let me stumble through and practice to get better. Instead, he would send me on an errand, take whatever I was working on, and finish the job for me while I was gone. As a young boy, that shouted out loud and clear to my inner critic that I was doing something wrong and that I wasn't good enough, or smart enough.

Last December, now in my late sixties while standing in my kitchen, it finally hit me that Dad's teaching style was one of the main reasons I had so much success in my coaching career. I thought about the way he taught me and how it made me feel, and how I wished there was another way, which I eventually found. With that realization, I stood in my backyard and had a talk with my dad, who had passed away in 1992.

"Dad," I began, gazing up toward the sky, "I want to truly thank you for teaching me the way you did." I let him know how much I appreciated him and that his teaching method was actually perfect, it caused me to teach with patience, compassion, and understanding. I let him know that without him I would have never become a USA National Team Coach and traveled all over the world with incredibly talented human beings! More importantly, I thanked him for helping me touch and change so many lives over my forty-six-year career. I know he heard me, because during the entire conversation my entire body was tingling and was covered with goose bumps. All the hairs on my arms and the back of my neck were standing straight up. I got the sense that he was pleased and proud of who I had become. As I was walking back in the house, I swore I heard him say, "You're welcome. It was what I signed up for." It was true confirmation for me to know and believe everything really does happen for a reason.

6

PINEWOOD DERBY

Like so many other boys in my neighborhood, I joined the Cub Scouts. We did all the things Cub Scouts do to earn badges and awards, but there was one event that had a huge impact on my life, the Pinewood Derby Race. It was the first time I had ever competed in an organized event. I learned very quickly about the relationship between detailed preparation and winning. More importantly, I learned that the journey was more important and enjoyable than the winning itself.

Everyone in our troop got a pinewood derby kit, which came complete with one pine block of wood, four plastic wheels, four nails for axles, two cross pieces of wood for the axles to fit into, and a handbook that included all the rules and regulations. Each boy, with the help of his mom or dad, had to design a car. The car could not weigh more than four and a half ounces, and we could not use any type of lubricant on the axles.

It was an amazing process working with my dad, transforming that block of wood into an actual Indianapolis style racing car. First, we had to decide on a design for the car. Then my dad drew lines on the block, so we knew where to plane, file, and sand. I wasn't sure how it was going to come out, but my dad had a vision and knew exactly how it was going to look per our discussion and decision about the Indy style body type. All I saw was a block of wood. I was fascinated with the step by step process.

The cool thing was that for the first time in all our projects together, my dad showed me how to do everything, and then he actually let me do it. I learned how to use a plane and a file for the first time. We put that block of wood into a vice and he showed me how to set the blade for the plane. He taught me how to use the plane and how you always go with the grain of the wood. After I had planed the wood down to the line we drew, he showed me how to form the front end of the car with the file. It was like a work of art. That block of wood became a racing car right in front of my eyes. The exciting part of this adventure was I was making it happen with the guidance of my father. We were doing it together.

Once we finished the hood and grille for the front half, it was time to shape the rear end of the car. In the early 60's, the Indy cars had a fin on the back end, so I asked my dad if we could make a fin. He said, "It's your car, you can design it any way you want," which was music to my ears. The rear end was a little harder to shape. I had to use a file to round off the back end of the block, and at the same time, leave a thin piece of wood for the fin. I couldn't just plane the wood down like the front end. It took me a long time to shape the back end of the car. Once I got the back end rounded just like we wanted it, I had to form the fin. This was the most delicate part of the operation. I had to use a fine file and be very careful not to use too much pressure. I started with the file, and then my dad suggested using sandpaper to form it just right.

Once we had the body of the car all formed, it was time to

form the cross bars that held the axles. We centered each crossbar in the cut-out slots on the bottom of the car. My dad had me mark lines on each side of the car, so I knew how much of the crossbar to form. He had me take the square pieces of wood and file the edges in a half round fashion on both sides. In the end, the cross bars looked like the front housing of Indy race cars. Then I had to sand the body and the cross bars to make everything smooth for painting. Before we painted, we had to attach the cross bars onto the bottom of the car. The wood was so fine and light that my dad thought that regular nails would split the wood, and we would be out of luck because you didn't get extra parts with the kit. He took straight pins from my mother's sewing kit and cut them in half with wire cutters and had me nail the crossbars on with them. It worked perfectly. As we finished each section of the car, he would weigh it to see how much more we should take off or have to add on so the car would weigh as close to the four-and-a-half ounces as possible. This was something that he kept his eye on the entire time we were building the car. He told me that we wanted the car to be as close to the maximum weight limit because a heavier car would build up more momentum and speed going down the track than a lighter car. We actually ended up drilling a hole in the bottom of the car and adding a round lead weight to reach the maximum legal weight level.

I watched in awe and curiosity as Dad added one last little trick. He took out his electric drill, mounted it on the workbench, and put the nail, aka the axle, into the drill, locking it down. He turned on the drill, and as the nail spun, he took a number 2 lead pencil and ran it up and down the shaft. He did that for each of the axles. It wasn't a lubricant, but he explained that the lead coating would make the nails slipperier so the wheels would spin faster. I was blown away. Not only did he know about aerodynamics for wind resistance, he had come up with an ethical and legal way to make the car go faster. He had thought of every little detail that would give us the best chance to win.

When the car was finished and painted, it looked just like an Indy car racer. It even had a roll bar that we made out of an old wire hanger. The day of the big race came, and our car won first place in our local troop. Two weeks later, we went on to win first place in the district finals against all the packs in northern California. It was one of the best experiences of my life, and as I said earlier, the journey was as much or more fun than the winning! I realized we won because of all the detailed thought and preparation we put into the design of the car and the elements that would give us the best chance to win. From this experience, I developed an eye for detail that I incorporated into my own gymnastics career and later in my coaching career. My being detailed oriented allowed all my athletes to win competitions, leading me to be invited on the coaching staff of the Women's USA National Team. Thank you, Dad!

7

UNICYCLES

It was the summer after my fifth-grade year when the entire family went to see the big Fourth of July day parade in the next town over from ours. I stood on the curb of the sidewalk next to my sisters in front of Mom and Dad, watching the high school bands, local homemade floats, and old cars pass by. Then I saw something I'd never seen before– a large group of kids, riding shining chrome bicycles with just one wheel and no handlebars! The shiny fancy sign that preceded the group said, "The Blue Devils." I turned for a second and looked up at Dad wide eyed, and he explained that the bikes were called unicycles and they were a competitive drill club from Concord. The very city we were in. I couldn't take my eyes off of their fancy uniforms and chrome unicycles with padded black seats. I stood on my tip toes and watched as they weaved in and out of each other without crashing. They could stop, turn on a dime, stay in one place, and even ride backwards. It was mind-boggling to me how they could maneuver a single wheel with no handlebars or brakes. In that moment, I knew I wanted to do what they were doing. I wanted to be a unicycle rider.

As soon as we got home, I asked my parents if I could get a unicycle. As I knew they would, they said we'd have to see how much one would cost. Sadly, I found out that unicycles cost as much or more than our house payment and my parents said we couldn't afford one. I sat out in the backyard on the stoop trying to hold back my tears. Eventually, my dad came out to join me. He put his arm around my shoulders, and I knew he was just as upset as I was that we couldn't afford a unicycle. We sat like that for some time, and as we did, my eyes surveyed the toys and tools in the backyard, and I felt an idea emerge. "Dad," I asked, looking up at his whiskered chin, "Could I build a unicycle?" A large smile spread across my dad's face, and before I knew it, we were standing in front of his tool bench, taking the wheel off my sister's old tricycle that was in the storage bin. It was perfect because a tricycle wheel has built in pedals with a fork and shaft that connected to the handlebars. Next, I had to figure out how to connect the seat to the wheel. I asked dad if he had any pipes that I could use as a stem to connect the wheel to the seat. He said, "You can use some of the aluminum tubing from the old clothesline we have lying around in the side yard." I grabbed the hacksaw bolted to the backyard and cut a piece of the tubing about two feet long. When I slid it over the shaft of the fork, it fit perfectly, as though it was meant to be. Then I drilled a hole through the tubing and the shaft of the fork, and I bolted them together. I found an old bicycle seat and clamp that was hanging up on the wall of the garage from one of our old bikes. I pried open the clamp, slipped it over the tubing, and stuck the neck of the seat into the top of the tubing, bolting it down. Just like that, I had a unicycle! It wasn't fancy like the ones the Blue Devils had, but it worked, and it was all mine. When I walked through the back door with my new prized possession, my dad smiled with pride, and Mom started clapping. My younger sister, on the other hand, wasn't impressed and had a few things to say about her old tricycle!

My pride quickly evaporated as I walked out the back door and realized I had a big problem to solve. How do I learn to ride this one-wheel contraption? I had no idea where to start. So, I started from the beginning! I got this idea I could build some parallel bars like therapists use to teach people how to walk again after an injury. I knew we had some long bamboo poles in the woodpile out back that would be perfect. We had a solid wood picnic table and benches on the patio that would make a great base for my parallel bars. I took the two bamboo poles and tied them onto the picnic table about shoulder width apart. I stacked the two benches on top of each other at the other end of the poles and tied them together, then tied the poles to the benches. I hooked the seat of the unicycle on top of the table so it couldn't move. That way I could mount the unicycle without falling on my face. I climbed onto the unicycle, grabbed a hold of the parallel bars, and started to peddle. I walked my hands along the poles inch by inch until I got to the other end. Then I would put both hands on one pole and turn myself around one quarter turn at a time until I pivoted back the way I came. It must have taken me hundreds, if not thousands, of laps before I was able to ride the entire length of the poles without touching them, but soon I was riding from the table to the benches, hands free. Next, I took both of the poles away, moved the picnic table to one end of the patio, and started to see how far I could ride without falling. Before I knew it, I was riding the entire length of the patio.

I still had to learn how to maneuver and turn this one-wheeled contraption. I kind of knew what to do from pivoting around between the parallel bars when I got to the end and wanted to go back to the table. I would turn the wheel by using my hips and shoulders, so I gave it a try. I found out quickly that you only needed to make minor adjustments to turn when you are moving verses being stationary at the end of the parallel bars. It was hard to judge time because I was having so much fun, but pretty soon, after a lot of falling, I could turn on a dime just like the kids in the parade.

I only had one major problem left to solve and that was how to get on the dang thing without the use of the picnic table. I flashed back to the parade and remembered seeing how the kids got back on their unicycles when they fell. They put the seat under their rear end, put the pedals parallel to the ground, and then stepped on one pedal to make the wheel go underneath them as they put their other foot on the opposite pedal to start riding again. It looked pretty easy when I saw them do it. It wasn't easy. The first time I tried to get on trying this so-called simple technique, I face planted onto the cement patio. I remember pushing the first pedal way too hard and missing the second pedal with my other foot as the unicycle catapulted underneath me like a bullet being shot out of a gun. I ended up on my stomach, and the unicycle ended up three or four feet behind me. So, mounting the unicycle obviously wasn't as simple as it looked. I had to come up with another idea. So, I used the outside wall of the house to put my hand on to balance and stabilize myself while I was trying to learn how much pressure to apply on the first pedal to get on this one-wheel death trap. Eventually, with a lot of practice, I learned the art of mounting a unicycle and was free to roam the neighborhood.

From that moment on, I spent hours a day riding my unicycle everywhere, to the store, my friend's house, even to the school yard. Neighbors would stare and clap as I rode down my street that summer. It was like being in my own personal parade. My unicycle journey was invaluable. I learned to use my imagination and creativity, overcome obstacles and setbacks, and most importantly not to take things at face value.

8

LEARNING TO DANCE

In the seventh grade, my school, Valley View Intermediate, hosted dances every month. The Beatles had just taken over America, and Hi-Fi stereo record players were the big craze. All the kids in my neighborhood were talking about how cool the dances were. I wanted to go, but I didn't know how to dance and thought that everyone would laugh at me if I tried.

I asked one of my dearest childhood friends, Marilyn Ingram, if she would teach me how to dance? She said, "No problem. It'll be fun." She lived one house up the hill from me, and we had been close since the second grade. I felt comfortable asking her for help with this awkward situation. Marilyn didn't have a shy bone in her body and was very confident. She also didn't take any crap from anyone.

The weekend before the dance, I went up to Marilyn's house, she put a stack of 45's on the stereo, and we proceeded to dance. Her long shining brown hair flipped and bounced off her shoulders and back as she busted a move. I guess the dumb founded look on my face forced her into action because she grabbed my hand, pulled me right beside her, and said, "Just do what I do." I knew better than to argue with her, so I mimicked her every move. I guess it's true what they say, the best way to learn how to swim is to jump into the deep end. Before I knew what happened, I was dancing. Her matter of fact approach worked miraculously.

I just had one major problem to overcome, my dreaded fear that everyone would stare and laugh at me at the dance. I confessed my fear to Marilyn. She said, "That's ridiculous. No one will even care or pay attention to you. They are all too busy thinking about themselves." I put on a brave smile and shook my head, but I didn't buy any of what she said. Course, I wasn't about to tell her that.

Friday night rolled around. I put on my freshly pressed Levi jeans, a button-down paisley shirt, and my new converse, and I went to the dance. Once I was there and everyone started to dance, that little voice in my head took over, and I just stood there like a wallflower thinking I had just made the biggest mistake of my young life. The next thing I knew, Marilyn came out of nowhere and said, "Let's dance."

I told her, "No!" As the word came out of my mouth, a chill ran down my spine and throughout my entire body because instinctively I knew what was going to happen next.

Sure enough, she grabbed my hand with a vice like grip and jerked me out onto the dance floor. I felt the blood rush out of my face, and my arms and legs felt like they weighed a ton as I stood there motionless. Her glaring beautiful green eyes, shrugged shoulders, arms spread out palms up, said loud and clear, "Start dancing if you want to live."

I sheepishly started to move my feet, constantly looking over my shoulder to see if anyone was laughing at me. Once I made a complete 360-degree scan of the room, I realized that no one was staring at me or laughing, just as Marilyn predicted. I let loose, put my whole body into it, and really started dancing. There aren't words to describe the joy that came over my body in that moment. I can't even begin to describe how much fun I had that night, not to mention the adrenaline rush of overcoming a fear.

That magical night was the start of a lifelong love affair with dancing that is still burning bright inside of me today. The love of dancing allowed me to meet my beautiful wife, Victoria, and create a life beyond my wildest dreams. I can't even imagine what my life would be like today if I hadn't had the courage and support of a great friend to overcome that anxiety. It's fun to connect the dots of your life and realize everything happens for a reason, even when it is something small like learning to dance.

9

TOO LITTLE TO PLAY SPORTS

That first day of high school, I was fourteen years old, four feet eleven inches tall, and weighed seventy-eight pounds. I walked down the hallway and a few seniors laughingly yelled, "Hey kid I think you are lost. The elementary school is down the street." That kind of set the tone for my entire freshman year. I got stuffed into garbage cans, and I was even pushed around and bullied for my lunch money. I lost my popularity status from intermediate school where I was small, funny, buck toothed, and so ugly I was cute. That wasn't even the worst part. I loved sports, but I was too little to play any of them. Too short for basketball, there was no soccer back then, the lightest weight in wrestling was ninety-five pounds which seemed like a monster man to me. Tackle football was out of the question; besides, I think the uniform weighed more than I did. I wasn't powerful enough for baseball or fast enough for track. As a kid growing up in our neighborhood, I played a lot of sports with my friends, and now I was the only one who wasn't on a team. I came home after school to an empty neighborhood day after day for months. I was losing all my childhood friends. So, when the announcement came over the intercom in first period one day that there was going to be open tryouts for the gymnastics team, I instantly knew this was my one and only opportunity to be part of a team.

I had been preparing for this moment for the past four years and didn't realize it. I had taught myself how to walk on my hands in the fifth grade after seeing a sixth grader walk all around the playground on his. In seventh and eighth grade, I took an early morning gymnastics class two days a week before school. I had to get up early and literally run over two miles just to be in the class because I lived in another city. The class was a total blast and at the same time very structured, disciplined, and organized. It was run by the vice principal of our school, Howard Mormon, who was the former gymnastics coach at the high school before taking the vice principal position. I learned how to flip forwards and backwards on the trampoline. I learned to do cartwheels, round-offs, and front and back handsprings on the tumbling mat. Being small, strong for my body size, and agile was a plus in this sport, and I excelled rapidly.

All that preparation paid off the day of tryouts. I made the varsity team as a freshman and was the first athlete in the ten-year history of the school to become a four-year letterman in any varsity sport! I reached regional and state championship status as an all-around gymnast which allowed me to pick and choose where I wanted to go to college. Being too small, which I considered a major flaw in myself, turned out to be a blessing in disguise. Often what we think is a weakness is actually an opportunity to discover our strengths, gifts, and talents in order to reach our full potential. I would have never guessed in a million years that being too small to play traditional sports would lead me to travel the world with Olympians.

10

MAURICE

I will never forget the first time I met Maurice Williams. Ray, our coach at Chico State University, had just recruited a whole new team of junior college transfers and two new freshmen. We were all moving into our new team house one late September day in 1970 when Maurice drove into the circular dirt driveway in a brand-new gold convertible Firebird, radio blasting, and his beautiful tall girlfriend beside him.

He was bigger than life. Although he was only five feet four inches tall, he had eighteen-inch arms and a fifty-inch chest. He was one big massive muscle. While introducing himself, completely crushing my hand, he jerked me in, got right in my face, smiled and whispered, "Stay away from me. I don't like you, and I would just as soon beat the shit out of you as be your friend." Not quite the start of a friendship I was hoping for.

As the days went by and we all got settled into the house, school and workouts, things were going fine. Until one day, I noticed that some of my food was missing from the refrigerator. I yelled out, "Who ate my food?" And of course, Maurice said, "I did, and I'll do it anytime I want to."

I had a big problem and had to figure out some way to solve it quickly. I couldn't afford to feed myself and him too. I knew I had to stand up to him, but how? Fighting him was pure insanity! Maurice had grown up on the back streets of Berkeley, fighting his whole life, and he was looking for any excuse to pound the crap out of me. So, after some thought, I came up with an idea. I decided to challenge him to a strength contest in the gym. I thought even if I can't beat him at least I could gain his respect...hopefully. The next day at practice, I stood up in front of the entire team and challenged Maurice to a strength contest. With a smirk on his face and a chuckle in his voice he said, "Bring it on." Ooh's and ah's flooded the gym as all of our teammates egged us on. Maurice asked, "OK what's the strength contest?"

I told him that we were going to do one hundred bar dips and then hold an iron cross on the rings for as long as we could. With all the electricity, excitement, and testosterone in the air, you could cut the atmosphere with a knife. As a unit we all marched to the parallel bars. Maurice and I set the bars, jumped up on opposite ends facing each, other and pumped off fifty bar dips. Since I was in charge of the contest, I set the pace, hoping to wear him out. I wanted to starve those big muscles of his of oxygen. So, within a matter of seconds I said, "Let's go!"

We jumped up faced off again and pumped off fifty more bar dips. Leading the pack, I marched toward the rings. He said, "I'll go first."

I shouted out, "No, I'll go first." I immediately jumped up on the rings, muscled up to support, lowered down into an iron cross and held it for ten full seconds. He jumped up lowered down to the cross position, and he held it for nine... ten...eleven...twelve...fifteen seconds.

I kept a good game face on, but internally I was jittery, anxious, and nervous. I did not know what to expect next. My answer soon came. Maurice said, "I can't believe how strong you are for such a skinny little guy!" He shook my hand without crushing it this time. Smiled and gave me the respectful manly head nod. With beads of sweat on my forehead, I thought to myself, *thank God, my plan worked!*

Not only did I gain his respect, but I also earned the respect of everyone on my team, including the coach. I don't think anyone knew how strong I was except me. Maurice and I became true friends over the years, and we are still friends today. I did what I always have done, since I was a little kid. I didn't let challenges and obstacles stop me. I used my creativity to figure out a way to get what I wanted. In this case, what I needed.

In any situation in life there is always a simple answer. It may not be apparent or easy. But if you keep an open mind and look for the simple answer, it'll show up.

11

PLANTING THE SEED

I had just completed my rotation on vault and had marched to my next event–parallel bars. Sitting in the waiting area at the 1971 San Jose State University Spartan Invitational, I saw my coach out of my peripheral vision running toward me wide eyed and grinning from ear to ear. He came to a screeching halt in front of me and blurted out, "Guess what Jim Turpin just told me." Jim Turpin was the current NCAA National Vaulting Champion and a World Class Trampolinist. He said, "Your boy, Buckmann, is a perfect candidate for the handspring front vault."

A handspring front vault was a highly technical multiple flipping vault that only two or three people in the country were trying at the time. My twenty-year-old ego perked up as I sat tall in my chair. With my chest puffed out, I pushed my hair back, looked up at Coach, and said, "No shit. Are you kidding?"

He said, "What do you think? Want to go for it?"

I yelled, "Hell yes!" And the egotistical journey of training this handspring front vault began.

12

TRAINING

The day after we got back from San Jose, I started training the vault. I had no clue or idea what I was getting into, but I didn't care. All I knew was that I was going to learn this vault, no matter what. Nothing was going to stand in my way. Jim Turpin's words had been ringing in my ears for the past day and a half. This vault was the only thing on my mind. My ego was in overdrive and my mind was on autopilot. All I kept hearing was, "Do you know what this vault will do for your career?"

It is amazing how powerful the ego is. In my case, it was so inflated that it overpowered any and all logical thinking. To compound the situation, the coach's ego and my ego were feeding off each other. I hung on his every word, faithfully trusting and following all of his instructions, even though I could sense he really didn't know what he was doing. There was no rhyme or reason to the training. It was the blind leading the blind. We were using the huck–n–chuck, trial and error method. I just kept telling myself, *when in doubt, go harder*. This enabled my conscious mind to not question the approach we were taking. On top of all of that, I was actually making progress and having little successes, which just clouded my decision making even more. I spent the next three weeks training the vault every day, most of the time landing on my butt, stomach, or back. If I attempted fifteen vaults in practice, I never landed more than one or two on my feet. I just thought that with more training, I would develop the kinesthetic awareness I needed to enable myself to land it all the time. What the hell was I thinking?

The weekend finally arrived for our first home meet where I was going to unveil the vault. In one aspect, I was totally psyched. I knew that the fans had never seen this vault before. On the other hand, I was petrified that I would crash and burn in front of six thousand people. Looking back on it now, this was an insane decision. I usually trained skills between three to six months before incorporating them into my routines, and I never trained new skills during the competitive season. I also wondered why it never dawned on me or my coach to have a conversation whether training this vault was a good idea in the first place.

The night of the meet, the gym was packed from floor to ceiling. I had nailed all my routines on the first three events. Vault was next. I paced the floor behind the row of chairs my teammates were sitting in, trying to harness my nervous energy. Standing off to the side of the vault runway, I closed my eyes and visualized myself doing the vault perfectly. When I opened my eyes, the green flag was raised, and I stepped on to the runway. I took a deep breath in, blew it out, and flew down the rubber pathway. I hit the springboard at full speed. As my hands made contact with the horse, I pushed downward, shoved my shoulders open as hard and as fast as I could, and tucked my legs to initiate the 1½ flip back to my feet. Through sheer determination, a lot of adrenalin, and the grace of God, I stood the vault up and stuck the landing. It was like I had been doing the vault all my life.

There was a tremendous vibration that reverberated throughout the entire gym as the crowd erupted! Internally, I couldn't believe what just happened. I saluted the judges, waved to the crowd and acted like this was normal procedure. I sprinted back towards my teammates who were running out to meet me and jumped into their outstretched arms. They knew what I knew; that nailing that vault was pure luck. The celebration was interrupted with an even bigger roar when the 9.5 score was posted. Not only was that a new school record, but I had improved my vaulting score by one full point in just three weeks. Still reeling from what just happened, I walked out to the center of the floor, took a bow and waived to the crowd to thank them. There was no turning back now. I was hooked!

13

THE DECISION

B eing an all-around gymnast with four upper body events to train, (pommel horse, still rings, parallel bars, and horizontal bar) the workouts took a toll on my body, especially my hands. I would get rips weekly. Rips are where your callused skin sometimes six layers deep, tears off in the palm of your hands and leaves a huge crater of open, raw, pink flesh.

I was having a grinder workout. It was one of those days when no matter how hard I focused, I couldn't hit a routine to save my life. Nothing was working! And on top of all of that, I had three quarter sized rips on both hands. I unbuckled my grips, threw them in to my gym bag, and kicked the bag across the floor. Just as my bag landed, my coach yelled, "We're going out to the main gym to vault."

Thank God!

I don't know why I thought that vaulting was going to be any better than the other events I managed to screw up on that day. I was just happy to get some relief for my raw hamburger hands. Intuitively, I knew I should have called it a day and went home. But in typical fashion, I ignored my gut feeling, taped my hands, and pushed on. I was focused and determined to turn this day around.

Every attempt I made to do this crazy vault ended with me flat on my back or flat on my stomach. After ten crash and burn landings, I stood at the end of the runway and paused to breathe, focus, and visualize. On my eleventh attempt, I took off on the wrong foot and decided to bail out of the vault. That's when I found myself flat on my back, paralyzed, looking up at the stunned faces of my coach and teammates.

Feeling nothing from the neck down my mind instantly went into freak out mode.

Is this the way I am going to be the rest of my life? How am I going to take care of myself? Will my girlfriend still love me? What are my parents going to say? What about school? Holy shit, I'm totally screwed.

Before I went off the deep end completely, my coach and teammates talked to me and brought me back into the moment. Coach mentioned that Tom, our trainer, was on his way. Nervously trying to lighten up the moment, one teammate admitted that when they first saw me land on my head they started laughing because it looked so funny, which actually made me laugh.

Not only was I in shock. I don't remember how much time passed until the sharp stabbing pain started. At that moment, I didn't know if I wanted to feel what I was feeling. The pain was intense and completely indescribable. I actually remember wishing that I couldn't feel anything like when I first woke up. The pain started at the base of my neck and went all the way down my back and into my legs. Tears ran down my cheeks and onto the mat as I buckled under the pain and reality of the situation. I had never experienced this type of pain in my entire life. It was a combination of pinpoint sharp pain at the base of my neck, and an intense dull aching throughout my entire back. The only positive from the pain was that I could feel my body again, except for my arms.

When Tom arrived, he performed palpitation tests and asked me a bunch of questions. Can you wiggle your toes? Yes. Can you move your fingers? No. Can you move your arms? No. He would pinch or scratch a certain body part and ask can you feel this? He quickly barked out an order for someone to go to the training room to get a neck brace, "Pronto." While we were waiting for the neck brace, he quizzed my coach on what exactly happened and how I landed. One of my teammates rushed back with the brace and handed it to Tom, he ever so gently secured the brace around my neck and continued to examine and question me. Then he asked the question I never expected; do you think you can get up off the floor by yourself? Being twenty and not knowing any better I told him I think so, mainly because that is what I wanted to believe I could do.

My 'never give up' attitude and ego were stronger than my common sense once again. If that wasn't stupid enough the next statement was the clincher. "I don't want anyone to help him up. I want to see if he can get up on his own." To show you how much I was out of it, I thought he wanted me to get up on my own to observe and evaluate how much damage was done to my body in order to give an accurate report to the doctor. I had taken Tom's, 'care of athletic injury and first aid course' and found him to be very knowledgeable so I trusted him. I didn't question his decision. I did, however, question my own decision very quickly. When I attempted to ever so gingerly roll to my right side to make it easier to sit up, my body rudely interrupted me with an excruciating piercing stabbing pain in my neck. The pain was accompanied by bolts of static electrically charged energy that zinged out the top of my head, the bottom of my feet, and every hair follicle on my body. The only way I know how to describe it is like when you hear static electricity on your radio, except it felt a thousand times worse than it sounds. Once on my side I had to use all of my core strength to sit up which brought tears to my eyes again. Sitting upright, I slowly inched my legs underneath me in order to stand up, all the time desperately wanting to use my useless dangling arms. I have no idea how long it took me to stand up, it felt like hours. My best guess would be twenty to thirty minutes. I actually ended up slowly walking out of the gym on my own power.

As I carefully shuffled across the gym floor on my way to the doctor's office, it took all of my mental and emotional strength not to start screaming, crying, and yelling. My mind started to run all kinds of scenarios of what my life would look like with paralyzed arms. Every single scenario sent shivers up and down my spine.

14

TRIP TO THE DOCTOR'S OFFICE

Driving in Tom's car to the team doctor's office I could actually feel the vibration of the tires as they rotated over the road. My short-circuited nervous system was on hyper drive. Whenever the car turned, stopped, or accelerated, my neural pathways would light up like a pinball machine. My back muscles were as tight as a snare drum, and I had no way to relax or get comfortable. I was one big bundle of hurt from the neck down, except for my arms.

When we arrived at the doctor's office, he took one look at me and said, "You need to see the orthopedic specialist down the street." So, I once again had to maneuver my way back to the car. I got in, which hurt like hell, and I took another excruciating, statically charged excursion to the next doctor's office. The team doctor called ahead so the orthopedic doctor was waiting for us. The reception nurse escorted me into a room and helped me lie down. The act of lying back down, although assisted, was nearly as painful as getting up on my own. My lifeless left arm was hanging off the side of the table with my raw palm facing up. When the doctor came in the first words out of his mouth were, "What the heck happened to your hand?"

"It's not my hand doc it's my neck." As he examined me, he asked a lot of questions. He then said, "We'll need x-rays to see what's going on."

So, for the third time, I had to get back up from a lying position and walk two doors down to the x-ray room. Good thing I was in shock and not questioning why no one, including myself, seemed to understand the risk I was taking every time I moved. Not to mention all the pain I had to endure with every minute movement. Thank God, I didn't have to lie back down again! The technician took the x-rays with me sitting up on a stool. The protective lead vest felt like it weighed four hundred pounds and sent shock waves throughout my body when he put it on me. I know that it only took minutes for him to take the X-rays, but it felt like an eternity. I broke out in a cold sweat from having to endure the intensified pain that the weight of the vest created on my spine, neck, and back. I was afraid that I was going to pass out before he finished. The technician finished taking the x-rays and said he would help me back to the exam table, which fortunately was right next to the x-ray machine. Preparing to move for the umpteenth time, I lifted my right leg and put my bare foot on the cold tile floor. As I went to move my left leg, I couldn't move it or feel it. Panicked I tried to move it again with no luck. I blurted out, "I can't feel my left leg. I can't feel my leg!"

I heard him say, "I'll get the doctor," as he bolted out of the room.

Sitting there all alone, my mind immediately flashed back to when I was twelve years old. I witnessed my grandmother having a stroke that paralyzed the entire left side of her body. *"Shit, my arms are already gone. Now my leg. What's next? Is it going to slowly spread through my entire body until I'm paralyzed from the neck down?"* Before my mind ran completely out of control the doctor and the technician rushed back into the room. I screamed, "My left leg is dead!"

The doctor came over, lifted my leg off the stool, and dropped it on the floor. Hearing the thud and not feeling the impact or the cold tile made the hair on the back of my neck stand on end. "Did you feel that?"

"Nope!"

The two of them instantly laid me down on the exam table. The doctor started doing tests on me. He kept asking me, "Can you feel this," over and over and over again.

I couldn't see what he was doing, but I knew it wasn't good because my answer was always the same, "NO."

Then the doc said he had to check the x-rays to see what was going on. Observing his facial expressions and body language, he seemed to be a little perplexed with my situation. I instantly flashed back to visiting my grandmother in the convalescent home. I remembered all the nurses having to take care of her every need until she died a year later. I told myself there is no way I am going to live like that…ever! *You might as well shoot me now.*

The doctor reentered the room. His news only added to my nightmare. He regrettably announced that my neck was broken. He went on to explain that the disc in between the sixth and seventh vertebrae was gone. It had disintegrated and defused into my body on impact. He went on to clinically explain that my seventh vertebra was cracked in half. In a somewhat uplifting voice, he mentioned, "There is good news. Your vertebral column is totally aligned due to your back muscles contracting to protect your spinal cord." Then in a matter-of-fact tone, he told me I needed to be admitted into the hospital immediately to be put into traction. The thought of moving again and possibly losing my other leg and becoming totally paralyzed made my stomach turn. Finally, a wise decision was made, and he told me he had called for an ambulance. Within a few minutes, two paramedics rolled in a gurney. They loaded me up, strapped me down, and rushed me to the hospital, red lights, sirens, and all.

15

FIRST HOSPITAL STAY

The ambulance stopped. The back doors flew open. The paramedics pulled me out. The gurney wheels extended, and they rushed me into the emergency room. A team of nurses met us and rushed me down hallways into a room. The paramedics and nurses worked together to transfer me to the bed. Quickly and systematically, they cut the clothes off my body and put me in one of those backless gowns that lets your ass hangout. A curtain divided the room. I wondered if anyone was on the other side and what they must be thinking. All of a sudden, a male nurse wheeled in a metal cart of equipment, filled with aluminum tubing, clamps, weights and ropes. He introduced himself and announced that he would be setting up a traction apparatus. The frantic pace, the clanging, the smell of alcohol and fear in the air fueled my inner chatter, *crap these guys aren't messing around. I must be really screwed up.*

Within minutes, the traction apparatus was assembled. One nurse stabilized my head and neck as another slipped the head gear over my head and under my chin. Then he ran the rope through the pulleys, attached the weights on the other end, clipped the rope onto the head gear and slowly allowed the tension of the weights to put traction on my neck and back. I could barely open my mouth to talk. The parade of nurses seemed to be never ending. As the nurse wheeled his cart out of the room, another one wheeled in an IV bag and said the doctor had ordered some pain medication. She swabbed my left arm, stuck a needle in, taped it down and started the drip. Within minutes, the pain subsided, and I finally took a deep breath and relaxed. My life had changed so dramatically in the last few hours that it was hard to believe it was all real. I was secretly wishing, actually hoping, that it was all just a bad dream. I wished that I would wake up and everything would be back to normal.

16

A KNOWING

It never even occurred to me to go home to have my parents take care of me. A deeper part of me knew that if I went home, I would never recover. It was clear to me that I needed to overcome the paralysis and the pain in my own way and on my own terms.

Two days after the accident my parents came to see me for the very first time. After talking to the doctor and seeing their one and only son suffering and lying helpless in a hospital bed, my mom asked me a question. She leaned over my bed and looked right into my eyes, "I guess I can't convince you to quit, can I?"

"No," I replied.

With tears in her eyes she kissed me, and she and my father left. It was her way of asking if I would come home so she could take care of me. I know it took every bit of that tough Iowa farm girl mentality to walk out that door. Thank God, I had parents that were strong enough to let me make my own decisions. Their first visit was also their last.

17

MY NEW REALITY

I must have dozed off. When I woke, I was all alone. I had no concept of time. It felt like the middle of the night, but I had no way of knowing. There was no more hustle or bustle, and the hallways were empty. The pain meds obviously had worn off because the pinpoint piercing pain in my neck woke me up. I was in a constant state of discomfort and pain. The only temporary relief came from the pain medication every four hours. After a while, my body wanted the meds every two hours.

Tears ran down my cheeks, and I couldn't even wipe them away. My mind spun and the inner chatter took over again. *What am I going to do? How will I take care of myself? Am I going to be like this the rest of my life? Will anyone ever love me again? Will I ever be able to do gymnastics again? Will I have to drop out of school? What about my coaching career, and on, and on, and on?*

Up to this point, everything I had accomplished in my life was through the physical and now all my physical abilities were gone. I was a twenty-year-old invalid. The nurses had to feed me, bathe me, dress me, and wipe my ass. All I could think was I'd rather be dead than paralyzed.

18

EARL

Earl was the grandfather I never had. The next day right after breakfast an elderly, wise voice from the other side of the curtain said, "Hello roomy. My name is Earl." It was impossible to turn towards his voice due to the traction. "Hello Earl, glad to meet you. My name is Gary." He was a God send that allowed me to put things into a whole new perspective and get through the daily grind of my current circumstances. I learned more in those two months than I ever learned reading any of my schoolbooks or any book for that matter! We talked about life, our families, where we grew up, our injuries, sports, and of course love. Another amazing perk of having Earl as my roommate was his beautiful wife who would always bring us home cooked goodies, which beat the hell out of the hospital food.

I would tell him about certain experiences that had happened to me over the course of my life. In his infinite wisdom, he would enlighten me about why my life unfolded the way it did. It gave me a whole new perspective about my life that would have never occurred to me otherwise. He talked to me about his younger years and what it had taught him. He gave me a whole new positive outlook on life.

One morning after breakfast, he announced that he was cleared to go walking and that I would be his first stop. I could hear the shuffling of his feet and the clanging of his walker as I cheered him on. "I'm almost there," he kept repeating.

When he finally leaned over my bed, we met face to face. He looked just as I had imagined. Short, round, gray haired, a little balding on top; he was a jolly fellow with a majestic smile! We laughed, as I watched him gently take my hand and shake it and say, "So glad to put a face with a voice finally." I told him that as soon as I could, I would go walking with him. I watched him push his walker out the door and disappear down the hallway. I shed a few tears of joy for him and many more tears of sadness for myself.

19

TODAY'S THE DAY

After four weeks of lying flat on my back with no improvement, my doctor came in and gave me some devastating news. "Gary, you're not responding to any of the treatments, and there's a good chance that you are going to be paralyzed for the rest of your life."

I immediately blurted, "I don't think so, doc. That's not my plan." I had a feeling deep down inside, a gut feeling, that I could heal myself. I don't remember much after that because my inner chatter went ballistic, overflowing with worst case scenarios. I could hear the muffled voice of my doctor talking, but it was just noise. It was like my mind had dropped a movie screen right down in front of me so I could watch the story of my life as a quadriplegic. As I watched in horror, I saw my mom spoon feeding me, brushing my teeth, shaving my face, combing my hair, dressing me, and wiping my ass. I would be chauffeured everywhere I needed to go, never to ride a bike, a motorcycle, or drive my car again. I saw myself sitting poolside in a wheelchair not being able to dive in and swim around. If I was lucky enough to have a wife, I would never be able to wrap my arms around her or be able to hold our baby in my arms. My stomach was churning like a cement mixer, my heart pounding out of my chest, and every cell of my body was flooded with fear.

Once the doctor left, I do remember telling the nurse not to let anyone in to visit me that day, not even my teammates. I laid motionless the entire day to sort out all the emotions that were flooding my body. It was the longest twenty-four hours of my life. I ended that twenty-four-hour self-induced pity party by following my gut and making a decision. I decided that I was going to heal myself. I had no idea how I just knew that was what I was going to do!

Without realizing it, I had already started my healing process the day after I arrived. Having nothing but time on my hands, lying flat on my back 24/7, staring at the ceiling (which by the way didn't even have any dots on it to count), I visualized. Day after day, week after week, I projected a new movie in my mind to see myself back to normal exactly as I was before the accident. Walking, hanging out with my teammates, and going to class every day. I saw myself competing again in front of 6,000 people in Acker gym at the university. I was dancing, partying, and going to football games. I saw my graduation and going on to my dream job. I saw myself coaching with my mentor and high school coach at his private gymnastics school. I was so detailed oriented that I saw the nerve impulses traveling from my brain through the neural pathways to my muscles, so I could move and feel them again.

Almost two weeks to the day that I got the devastating news, all my visualization paid off. Like clockwork, everyday one or more of my teammates came in to visit and support me. Today, it was Robert who showed up. This was perfect because Robert and I had formed a very close relationship. We were like brothers. Maybe it's because we were both born in December and were both Sagittarius.

As Robert came through the doorway, I said, "Today is the day."

With his head cocked looking at me sideways he asked, "Today's the day for what?"

"Today is the day I am going to move my leg."

"Really?" he exclaimed.

I told him to pull the sheets up off my feet. I told him I was going to try to wiggle my toes and to let me know if they move. He pulled the sheets back and said, "Let's do it."

I took a deep breath, like I did before performing any of my routines, and said, "Here goes."

"Yes, they moved" he yelled.

I said, "I'm going to do it again to make sure it wasn't just a muscle twitch." I took another deep breath and did it again. They moved.

The next thing I know we're both screaming and yelling. I started franticly kicking both my legs up and down in the bed. Yelling, "I got my leg back, I got my leg back, I got my leg back!"

The nurses rushed in to see what all the commotion was. Still yelling, I wiggled my toes and lifted both legs for them to see. They immediately called for the doctor. After examining me, he had no explanation for what had occurred, except to say, "It's a miracle."

In that moment I knew that if the nerve impulse went all the way down to my toes, I was surely going to get the use of my arms back some day. The next morning, I took my first of many walks with Earl like I promised. Two weeks later, the doctor released me from the hospital. Although my arms were still paralyzed, they said there was nothing more they could do for me.

20

TEAM HOUSE

After eight weeks of lying in a hospital bed, my release day finally arrived. I now had a neck brace instead of traction. All of my teammates, who were also my roommates, showed up to chauffeur me home. A nurse wheeled in a wheelchair, smiled, and asked, "Ready to go home?"

"I am beyond ready!"

The guys snatched up all my stuff, and we paraded down the hallway towards the entrance. We made one last stop at the pharmacy to pick up my pain medication. The nurse gently placed the bag full of pills in my lap and wheeled me to the entrance of the hospital, wished me good luck, and waved goodbye.

As the front doors slid open, I took in a breath of spring air. I smelt trees, flowers, pollen, and fresh cut grass. The warmth of the sun touched my face and the fresh air gently blew through my hair. It was a delightful contrast to the hospital environment, and I made sure to take it all in. Up ahead and to the right, I noticed a garbage can and told Robert to toss my bag of pills into it. I would have done it myself, but having paralyzed arms made it virtually impossible. I had become way too dependent on the pain medication, and I was afraid of becoming a drug addict. A few hours later, I was not a happy camper.

Being reunited with the guys and back in the real world, I felt almost normal again. The guys tossed my stuff in the trunk and five of us loaded up in Tim's tan Volvo. They let me ride shotgun with Maurice leading the parade on his motorcycle. As I walked through the front door of our team house, I passed through the living room full of backpacks, books, clothes, notebooks, bean bag chairs and into the kitchen filled with dirty dishes. I made my way to the staircase that led to my room. It was quite a contrast to the sterile environment that I had been living in. It felt good to be back in the animal house environment of our home.

Now my teammates were my nurses. They had to feed me, dress me, and yes, help me go to the bathroom. Thank God I got to shower in the locker room at the college after practice. My teammates were amazing. They didn't treat me any different than they did when I was healthy. They kept things light by mimicking me, joking around, and giving me a lot of crap. For example, when I would ask if anyone had seen my psychology book, they would swing one of their arms from their shoulders like they were paralyzed and point wildly at the other side of the room and say I think it's over there. It would always make me laugh. They also made eating very entertaining! Sometimes they would make a game out of feeding me. They would keep score of how many times they could fling food into my mouth from across the table. I got fed, but I looked like I had been in a food fight. To be fair, they took great care of me. Not only did they encourage me and support me, they also gave me tough love when I lost my way. Any time I started whining or having a pity party, they would call me on my shit. They straight up let me know they weren't going to listen to any negative crap. Their twenty-year-old mentality, energy, and compassion were always the perfect medicine I needed.

21

GETTING THE NEWS

E very night I would sit on my bed and flop one of my arms up into my lap and mentally try and move my fingers. Head shaking and body quivering, my eyes focused on my hand and I would silently repeat, *move, move, move, just move dammit*. I did this faithfully for several months.

My doctor was having me come in to see him every two weeks, when he wasn't cancelling my appointments because of surgery. After two months, I got tired of hearing the same old prognosis and diagnosis about why I still couldn't feel or move my arms. So, I stopped going to the doctor.

I already had my own healing regime. I had to drop out of school, and I spent all of my days, visualizing, walking, jogging, and going to the gym and the pool with the guys. I felt like I was doing all the right things to heal myself. In my mind I was moving in a positive direction and didn't need the doctor's negativity. I maintained this regime for the next three months.

One early September morning, I woke up to a very foreign sensation. I was pain free. For the past seven months I had learned to zero out the pain and discomfort of my neck and back. I was in a constant state of contraction and spasm. But this morning was different. Completely baffled, I took a few moments and some deep breaths to enjoy this unusual sensation that I had literally forgotten about. I didn't know how to react. On one hand, I was doing back flips in my mind. On the other hand, I wondered, *what the hell, how can this be possible?*

Perplexed, I decided to have one of my teammates dial the number of my doctor and hold the phone to my ear while I made an appointment. I wanted to know if he had an answer for this phenomenon. The only appointment available was the late afternoon, during workout time. So, I had to have a friend of mine drive me to the appointment. The next day at my appointment I wasn't greeted with normal bedside manner. "Where the hell have you been? Why didn't you keep your scheduled appointments? How the hell do you expect me to help you if you never show up?"

In retaliation, I retorted, "I got tired of hearing the same old story, so I've been out trying to heal myself." Without skipping a beat, I went on to explain that my back and neck muscles finally relaxed and that I was pain free. But as you can plainly see my arms were still non-operational.

True to form he responded with, "We need to take some x-rays."

My inner critic scoffed, *fine go ahead take your stupid x-rays.* Waiting for the doc to come back, I anticipated good news.

With X-rays in hand, the first words out of his mouth were, "You need an operation immediately."

"Whoa, hold up! What are you talking about? Why do I need an operation?"

He put the x-rays up on the monitor and waved me over. Being a physical education major, I had taken anatomy and knew what a normal vertebral column should look like. My seventh cervical vertebra had a huge crack in it, and was protruding out like a stair in a staircase. If that wasn't enough, the shock of seeing a finger sized bone spur growing out the front end of it made me feel like I was going to throw up. The doctor asked me if I knew how big a millimeter was. He said that my vertebra was hanging on by a millimeter or two. "If it slips off, it will sever your spinal cord, which will either kill you or make you a quadriplegic for the rest of your life. It could be something as simple as someone coming up from behind you, slapping you on the back to say hello. The vertebra would slide off, sever your spinal cord, and you would go down and never get back up."

The deliberate and somewhat spiteful picture he painted, gave me an empty, aching feeling in the pit of my stomach. I couldn't believe what I was hearing. "You mean to tell me that all this time it's gotten worse instead of better, and now I'm a walking time bomb and could die?" I wanted to throw my arms up in the air and scream more than a few profanities. I sat there pale and motionless.

My original x-rays showed my vertebra was broken but in perfect alignment because the back muscles spasmed and contracted to protect my spinal cord. Now that my muscles had relaxed, the bone slipped back into the original state of the initial injury and the fracture hadn't healed. I wanted to know what was up with the bone spur growing out the front of my neck. He explained it was where the body was trying to heal itself. "We need to schedule your surgery within the next day or two."

I told him I had to talk to my parents and let them know what was going on. I would call him tomorrow.

My eyes glazed over, and I walked right past my friend in the waiting room towards the front door. She intuitively knew to be quiet. She got up and opened the door. Side by side we walked a few blocks to a nearby park. We sat on the grass, and I started bawling. With her fingers she gently brushed the tears from my cheeks, lips, and chin. Using four letter superlatives, I barked out the whole scenario of my situation. Screaming and mumbling, I rambled on for an hour or more. I regurgitated all the things I had been doing for the past five months to heal. I cringed at the thought of jumping off the diving board, bouncing on the trampoline, and jogging three to four miles a day. Anyone of those activities could have killed me, or worse paralyzed me for life. I don't recall what she said to me, if anything, but her support was exactly what I needed. After all my ranting and raving, we walked back to the car and went home.

By the time we got there, some of the guys were already home from practice, and I quickly filled them in. "No problem. Whatever it takes, we'll be there."

I had someone dial up my parents. The conversation was short and sweet. We agreed that I should have the operation and they would drive up to be with me. In the morning, I informed the doctor of my decision, and he scheduled the surgery for the following day.

22

FIRST WALK

The temperature was in the triple digits. I hobbled and limped along the roadside on the first walk after my surgery. The procedure I had was called an anterior fusion. It's when the surgeon cuts a piece of bone about the size of a nickel out of your iliac crest (your hip bone) and inserts it in between the vertebrae in your neck. Then you have to wear a neck brace for six months while the bones grow together to become one solid vertebrae. I don't know if you have ever had a bone bruise injury before or not. They are very painful and take a long time to heal. Think of a time when you smacked your shin really hard into a piece of furniture or got kicked. Remember how your bone ached and how painful and tender it was to touch. Magnify that tenfold and you can imagine how much pain I felt in my hip. Now I had a new pain to zero out and heal. I had to wear elastic waisted pants for nearly a year.

My teammates and coach were in Los Angeles for a week, participating in the Santa Monica Gym Fest. So, my oldest sister, Gail, and her boyfriend came up and stayed at the team house to take care of me. It was great to get some TLC from my sister along with home cooking.

The only way to heal the bones in my hip and neck was to walk every day as prescribed by my doctor. The day after my operation an orderly made me get up and walk around my bed which made me break out into a cold sweat. By the end of the week, I was hobbling the length of the hallway and back. So, being an athlete, I took it to the next level and decided to walk a mile my first day out. Seemed like a good idea at the time. I don't know if my doctor would have approved of my decision.

During my walk, three different cars stopped to ask me if I needed help. Surprised and a little shocked, I would smile and say, "No thank you, I'm fine. This is just part of my therapy to help heal my hip." I was so focused I didn't take into consideration just how pathetic I looked. All I had on was a pair of gym shorts, tennis shoes, and a neck brace. My skin was lily white; my hair was greasy and messed up, and my body had atrophied away to just skin and bones. All of the vertebrae in my back were exposed as well as my ribs. My arms looked like two noodles hanging motionless by my sides. I looked like an escapee from a concentration camp. I would have stopped and asked if I needed help too.

This was the first of many walks which eventually turned into jogging. By consistently walking every day and increasing the distance, the doctor told me I was a month ahead of schedule in my healing process. This was one time my *never give up attitude* paid big dividends and worked for me and not against me. The extra blood flow and movement from walking helped the bone heal faster. The nice thing about taking things to the next level is it pays off in the end. So, when in doubt push the limits of what you think you can do.

23

BREAKTHROUGH

Two months of daily walks, leg and core exercises, visualizing, going to appointments, mentally and emotionally trying to move my fingers, I still had zero progress with my arms.

I was almost at the end of my rope. When one day on a routine walk, I noticed that my arms where swinging and I felt the cold November air on my hands. I stopped dead in my tracks. Wide eyed, heart racing, I gasped for air. I took a few deep breaths to focus and get centered like I did for competitions. I intentionally lifted my right arm and put it back down, then my left. I bent both arms ninety degrees, rotated my forearms for the first time in nearly a year, and with a simple thought my fingers moved.

My eyes welled up with tears, as I threw my arms up into a victory salute and pranced in a circle all the while screaming, "Yes, I'm back, I'm back. Thank you, God. I'm back!" I effortlessly wiped my tears with my coat sleeve, which brought a smile and more tears. I was in sensation heaven. I took in and instantly became aware of touch, pressure, heat, cold, texture, all of the sensations I took for granted. I made a vow to myself right then and there that I would never ever take my body for granted again.

I was walking on air as I made my way back home. As I was floating, I decided to get a little payback on some of the guys. My cockiness stemmed from knowing they couldn't physically mess with me in my condition. Already used to their verbal shenanigans, I felt pretty safe with my payback ploy. It took every ounce of concentration to contain my excitement and wipe the silly grin off my face. I kicked the bottom of the front door a couple of times which was my way of knocking and waited anxiously for someone to let me in. I kept my arms motionless as I walked into the house. Four of my teammates were in the front room. Rick unzipped my jacket, took it off and threw it on the couch. I started to walk towards the kitchen turned around and while pointing to my jacket with my right hand said, "Hey Rick can you hand me my jacket?" At the same time, I rubbed my nose with the back of my left hand. Rick yelled, "Did you just move your fucking arms?"

All heads turned towards me and time stood still like in a movie scene.

"Oh, you mean, did I point to my jacket like this and rub my nose like this? Yeah, I guess I did move my fucking arms."

Instantly the four of them surrounded me yelling, screaming profanities, and commanding me to move my arms some more. I'm pretty sure they wanted more proof before they started their celebration dance. In typical wild man fashion, we danced around the entire house. After whooping it up awhile, a miraculous sense of accomplishment and relief swept over us all. Deep down inside we all knew that what happened to me could have happened to anyone of us. This had been a team effort from day one, and finally we had a major breakthrough that we silently took in. It was a great victory!

A couple more stepping stones, and I would be home free. All I had left to do was get all of my strength back and regain all of my fine motor skills in my hands. Two challenges I joyfully looked forward to taking on.

24

OPERATION COMEBACK

I wasted no time in assessing my upper body strength, mobility, and dexterity. I started with simple tasks, like trying to make a fist, which was a no go. I tried to touch my thumb to my index finger, which was another no go. Sitting on a wooden chair, I attempted to push down with both arms to see if I could support my body weight. I might as well have tried to move a mountain. I was able to loosely clutch the receiver of the phone with both hands which sent chills up and down my spine. I still couldn't dial the rotary phone, but with help, I was able to get the doctor's office on the line.

Now that I had a starting point, my first goal was to get all of my fine motor skills back. My independence was my motivation. I couldn't wait to feed myself, comb my hair, tie my shoes, dress myself, zip up my pants, and all the little things that we all do without even thinking.

The next day at the doctor's office, my jaws ached from my permanent ear-to-ear grin. The doc had no explanation for my phenomenal recovery. I loved listening to him stumble and stammer about what he thought might have happened. It didn't really matter what he said because I knew the truth of why it happened. It was the power of mind over matter, positive thinking, visualizing, being persistent, consistency, and having an amazing support team.

People who have heard my story always ask me, "How did you know how to heal yourself?"

My response, which consistently caused head tilting and blank confused looks was, "I learned not to take *no* as a final answer at a very young age."

During my childhood, when I asked my parent's for things, the standard answer was no. "You can't have that. We can't afford it. That's not possible," or, "Get your head out of the clouds." So, I always looked for and found a way to get what I desired. Being paralyzed was no different in my mind. Being discouraged was motivation for me to discover another avenue to achieve the impossible.

By the time my appointment ended, I had a small squishy ball to squeeze, with type-written instructions. That ball became like another appendage of my body. I also had to work on touching the tip of my thumb to the tips of my fingers until I could rhythmically do it forwards and backwards. I spent the next eighteen months retraining myself and regaining all of my upper body strength. Over those months, I slowly got back to gymnastics training.

By the end of my recovery journey, I was actually stronger than I was before the accident. I was completely back and cleared for competition. The 1974-75 gymnastics season, my senior year, was the best and most enjoyable season of my entire competitive career. Oh, by the way, if you were wondering if I ever did the vault that broke my neck again, the answer is yes.

25

PERFORMING FOR THE CROWD

There were no competitive age group programs in sports when I was a kid, except little league baseball. I had no competitive experiences prior to high school. So, no one ever helped me understand how to handle the pressure of competition. I just trained to the best of my ability and figured that the winning part would eventually take care of itself. Unfortunately, it doesn't work that way.

There is a myriad of mental and psychological factors that come into play in any sport, but especially in the sport of gymnastics. You not only compete against the people on the other team, you also have to compete against your own teammates for individual awards. All eyes are on you, and there is no one to blame when you make a mistake. Today, sport psychologists earn a good living helping athletes understand and handle high-pressure situations. I wish someone would have helped me understand how to handle the pressure. It would have made my competitive career a lot more fun and successful.

It wasn't until my senior year in college that I figured out what kind of mindset I needed to compete at the highest level. That new perspective alleviated all the self-made pressure that caused me to be inconsistent. Gymnastics was the number one sport at Chico State, and we had sold out crowds of 6,000 plus for all our home meets. Sitting on the floor exercise mat stretching and warming up at the first home meet of the year, I paused to look around at all the people coming through the doors and filling the bleachers. I pondered, why do all these people come to watch us? In that moment it hit me. They came to see us do things they thought were impossible. They came to be entertained and amazed at the same time. It had never occurred to me what we provided for our audience before; we actually brought joy and happiness to our fans.

In that very same moment, I decided from there on out I was going to perform all my routines for the crowd. That simple decision gave me a whole new perspective and changed the course of my competitive season that year. By simply letting go of the competitive mindset and being of service to the crowd who came to watch and have fun, I was able to relax and perform my routines. I won three major competitions on the west coast, competing against Division 1 Pac-12 schools. I was the Far Western Conference All-Around, Floor Exercise, Vaulting, Still Rings and Horizontal Bar Champion. I also led our team to a fifth-place finish in the NCAA National Championship meet. Best of all, I was having fun and winning at the same time. That is what sports should be all about.

When you let go of your own agenda, be of service to others, and do what is fun for you that will always be a winning combination. There is always a simple answer for everything we just need to develop an awareness of that fact.

26

TEACHING WILLIE'S CLASS

Willie Simmons was my favorite professor in college. He was this tough, grey haired, slight of build New Yorker who was a former boxer. He had this direct no nonsense style of teaching, and at the same time, he was kind, caring, and compassionate. He taught me more about teaching than any other person in the world. My senior year Willie asked me if I would come in to one of his classes, Physical Education for the Adolescent, to be a guest teacher. He wanted me to teach a gymnastics lesson so his students would get a hands-on classroom experience of teaching young kids. He requested that I bring in one of my young gymnasts from the Chico Gymnastics Center where I was currently coaching. My college coach started the center my junior year and gave me a job, knowing I had coached in high school. I told Willie, "No problem. I have the perfect kid, Courtney, who just happened to be the daughter of the assistant football coach at Chico State.

The day of the class, we were in the main gym at the university with fifty or sixty college students looking on. Courtney was this three-foot, thirty-two pound, dark haired, brown eyed, olive skin, strong, confident, five-year-old dynamo. Willie told his students that he would be intermittently stopping my lesson to point out important teaching techniques that were not in their books. The first thing I did was to walk over to Courtney and explained to her the sequence of skills she was going to do. As I stood up, Willie shouted out and asked his students, "Did you see what just happened here?" My heart dropped and my mind immediately uttered, *great you haven't even started, and you already screwed up*. All the shaking heads and blank looks on every student's face, including mine, clearly indicated we didn't have a clue what he was referring to.

He went on to explain that a number of very important things just occurred during my talk with Courtney. "Did you notice how he squatted down to be at eye level to talk with her instead of standing over her and talking down at her?" He also explained how that single gesture creates a teacher student relationship that instills trust and confidence, which allows for effective and efficient learning. Then he asked, "Did you notice how he talked to her and the age-appropriate language he used?" He went on to point out how that the combination of the language and not talking down at her, established a mutual respect between the two of us. He said, "If he asked her to run through that wall over there right now, she would do it." I was shocked to have zero awareness of any of the positive points he was pointing out. I didn't even realize I did any of those things because I do them so naturally without thinking about it. It's our natural gifts that we don't realize we are doing that make us all unique and special.

Now you can see why I love Willie. He is a master teacher of the simple things that make a huge difference. I thought I was going to be teaching the students about gymnastics and instead we all learned some valuable lessons on being aware of all the little things that make teaching a magical tool to transform people's lives. The simple take away for me that day was to consciously incorporate all those techniques in my coaching career and pass them onto the students and other coaches.

27

KNEW WHAT I WANTED TO DO

S ince I was sixteen years old, I knew what I wanted to do for a living. In 1968, my sophomore year of high school, I was offered a coaching position at Diablo Gymnastics Club. My high school coach and mentor, Jim Gault, was the founder and owner. He obviously saw something in me that I hadn't seen in myself. I am so grateful that he did. I worked part time, Tuesday and Thursday from 6pm until 9pm, and from 9am to 12pm on Saturdays. Over the next two years, I fell in love with teaching and the potential of having an exciting career doing what I loved.

June 1970, Coach quit teaching at the high school and went full time into the private club business. Together with some of the parents of our gymnasts, he built and opened a brand-new facility in an old hardware store in Pleasant Hill. I worked full time that summer, and I saw firsthand what could be accomplished if you owned your own business. I was totally hooked. The day before I left for college, Coach grabbed me by the shirt, stared me straight in the eyes, shook me a couple of times, and told me that when I graduated there would be a job waiting for me. "So, don't forget to come home!"

In college, I majored in Physical Education but had little interest in getting my teaching credentials or working in the school system. I knew I wanted to run and own my own gym some day. Friends and family repeatedly told me I was crazy. Without my teaching credentials, I would never get a decent job. I wanted to teach in the private club system where students actually wanted to learn what I was teaching. I didn't want to deal with all the restrictions and bureaucracy of a school board. I'd be free to teach when I wanted and how I wanted. I'd be able to purchase the latest and greatest equipment that would enable students to have the best environment for learning. So, after five years of college, I graduated with a Bachelor of Arts degree in Physical Education, no teaching credentials and no job waiting for me at home.

During my absence, Mr. Gault was forced to hire an assistant coach to accommodate all the new growth of his business. Mr. Hal Shaw had my dream job and was well established in the company. Coach called me after graduation and regrettably informed me that my position had been filled.

I ended up staying in Chico and working at the Chico Gymnastics Center. My college coach promoted me to be the director and head coach of the center. I was doing what I loved but not where I wanted. Eight months later, Mr. Gault called me and reported that Hal moved back home to the Midwest and that my job was waiting for me if I still wanted it. Grinning from ear to ear, I packed up my bags and was soon back where I was supposed to be.

28

LEARNING HOW TO SPOT

I had been thinking about this moment every day for six years, and now it was finally here. I was thrilled and nervous at the same time. I knew this was where I was supposed to be, but within a day or two on the job, I discovered that I had a huge problem. I was missing one major skill I needed...spotting. I didn't know how to spot all the high-level skills the girls were learning and performing. I had walked into a nationally ranked high-level gymnastics school with virtually zero spotting skills. I was a highly skilled technician that could break down skills and teach them. I just had no way to manually assist the students to learn the skills safely. The pit of my stomach would knot up at the thought of going to work every day. I would wonder what skill I would have to spot, knowing that kid's lives were virtually in my hands. I of all people in the world didn't want to be responsible for hurting anyone. My injury became the motivation and turned into my big *WHY* in my coaching career. I was never ever going to let one of my gymnasts get hurt and suffer the way I did! This burden was almost too much to bear, and I thought my career would be over before it got started.

Instead of collapsing under the pressure, I decided to learn how to spot these high-level skills quickly and safely in my off hours. The simple answer presented itself when I thought about the little five and six-year-old developmental girls. They were strong, little, and light, which would allow me to manipulate them through the skills safely. I started flipping and twisting these little tiny tots, knowing that if I made a mistake, I could grab them mid air and save them before they hit the ground. Of course, I cleared it with Mr. Gault and their parents first. I spent hours before the team practice every day learning how to spot. I am happy to report that I never dropped one of the little developmental girls once. Soon I was enjoying my dream job instead of dreading it. When something is important in your life, it is worth it to face all obstacles and challenges that stand in your way head on. I learned that when I wanted a unicycle.

29

BUILDING THE GYM

I n the summer of 1978, Mr. Gault signed a ten-year lease for a 14,500 sq. ft. space in an old warehouse building in San Ramon, California. The entire building was 200,000 sq. ft. and was being sub-divided into individual business spaces.

The new state of the art Diablo Gymnastics School was scheduled to open the second week in September. We had planned everything out in detail from timetables of construction to the day we had to move out of the old gym. The only thing we didn't account for was the city of San Ramon taking their sweet time to approve the zoning status, so all the new companies could legally operate their businesses. The city approved the new zoning status two weeks before our opening day.

Not only did the building owner have to sub-divide the building, we, meaning me along with twelve dads, had to construct our entire floor plan for the gym. Additionally, we had to move all the equipment from our old gym and set it up. In a fourteen-day period we had to build office space, a locker room, two L shaped in-ground foam filled training pits the size of swimming pools, two raised 40 ft. x 40 ft. floor exercise platforms, a wooden retractable floor to go over the vaulting pit, a second story observatory, a 50 ft. long by three foot high barrier wall, paint the entire gym, and last but not least, drill twenty-eight anchor holes into the cement floor to secure all the equipment.

The main challenge we faced was the construction of the two in-ground pits. It involved a lot of demolition and major construction at the same time. First, we had to cut the 12 in. thick cement floor, then jackhammer all the cement out and remove it. Then dig the 4½ ft. deep swimming pool size holes and pour a new cement floor. We also had to construct new walls and completely pad all of the walls with 2 in. solid foam padding. We had everything covered except how to dig the holes. None of us knew how to operate a backhoe.

I thought I could learn how to operate it by the good old trial and error method. Running a backhoe is an art form. There are six different levers that all performed specific movements that directed either the scoop bucket or the arm for digging. The whole system was hydraulic, and you had to be able to move two or more levers simultaneously to have the arm and the bucket work together. It was like playing a keyboard on a piano. After an hour or so of swearing and breaking the back window of the load truck, I gave up.

I had to go downtown to the hardware store to get some more supplies. On my way, I passed a PG&E crew with a backhoe operator working on the side of the road. I decided to stop and ask for some tips and tricks on how to run the backhoe. I told the guy about my attempting to dig and the time crunch I was under. He said, "Well, I am an independent contractor. I don't work for PG&E, and I will be done here in about an hour. I could come over and take a look and let you know how long and how much."

I told him where we were located, and he showed up about an hour and a half later. He told me it would take him about four hours to do the job and it would be $200.00. I hired him on the spot. I couldn't believe how gracefully and fast he dug both pits. He was like an artist creating a master sculpture. Not only did he finish in four hours, he scraped the sides of all the walls to line up perfectly with the cement cut outs.

We worked eighteen-hour days from six a.m. to midnight for two weeks. We even had a friendly bet going on between us and the professional carpenters to see who would finish first. It created a fun competitive atmosphere that kept us motivated to work faster and more efficiently. It was like watching a finely choreographed dance routine. Everyone knew their jobs and the exact sequence in which they were supposed to perform them. We were in perfect rhythm moving from one project to the next never missing a beat. It was magical to experience.

I believe that the universe pitched in and helped us with the backhoe situation and the moving dilemma.

Oh yeah, I forgot to mention that one of our fathers in the gym had his own moving company. He donated his 50 ft. truck and an entire crew to move all the equipment from the old gym in one day. It was a cohesive and collaborative team effort on a daily basis. Not once did anyone complain or blame or criticize a fellow worker. Instead everyone just had positive input and solutions for any and all challenges and obstacles we faced.

We finished the morning of September tenth–our opening date. The simple answer for us doing the impossible was teamwork. We all had the same intention and determination to complete the job on time. We asked for help when we needed it and helped each other with our own gifts and talents to solve any and all challenges we faced. It reminded me of another impossible challenge I once faced.

30

THE BASICS

There were a lot of factors that contributed to my coaching system but none more pivotal than breaking my neck. My injury was totally preventable, and it changed my whole perspective on gymnastics and life. Lack of awareness was the reason I got injured because I skipped basic steps in my training. I didn't even realize that I was in trouble until it was too late to save myself. It took my thirst for knowledge to a whole new level. It woke me up and made me aware that I needed to develop a safer and more efficient way of training. From that rude wakeup call, a foundational, sequential, progressive, step by step basic program was born. It was a program designed and based on repetitive drills and lead-up skills to ensure that my students would not only mentally understand the concepts of the sport but develop total body awareness in order to safely perform a skill at the same time. My goal was to make sure that my students knew as much or more about the sport than I did.

We have all heard the saying, "We need to get back to basics," and that doing the basics is the key to success in life. The problem is most of us haven't accepted that statement to be true. The reason most of us skip the basics is they are boring, no fun, a pain in the butt, and time consuming. But they are so necessary to reach one's full potential.

I was always honest and up front with my students. I let them know exactly what they were getting into with my program. The way I combated the boring, pain in the butt, no fun, time consuming factors, during those tedious drills was to go ballistic about the smallest little detail of progress they made. I would jump up and down, wave my arms and scream, "That's it!" like they had just done a double twisting double back.

It's important to make the basics super exciting in order to keep your athletes motivated to enable them to actually learn the big skill. What most of us fail to understand, is that basics actually save time in the long run. I learned that lesson the hard way. Skipping the basics only allows athletes to reach a certain plateau in developing a skill or goal. Spending time initially to do the basic repetitive drills to develop total awareness, allows one to master any skill or goal.

I observed a few things over the decades that basics develop, not only in gymnastics but in both life and business; total body awareness to make adjustments and corrections, speed specific strength to perform skills, mental and emotional toughness to handle obstacles and challenges, overall knowledge that eliminates fear and instills confidence, consistency and repeatability.

During my coaching career, numerous coaches from all over the world would ask me the same question over and over, "How did you get your kids so strong?"

My answer was always the same, "We do a lot of basics."

With an "are you kidding me" facial expression, the comeback comment was always, "No, really how did you get your kids so strong?"

I would look them straight in the eye and repeat, "I make them do a lot of basics!"

They would throw their hands up in the air and utter, "Fine you just don't want to tell me so you can keep the secret all to yourself."

I would then explain to them the sequence of drills I had my kids do on an individual event and the amount of repetitions of each drill. I told them how many days a week we trained basics and how many months of the year we dedicated to basics. Once they saw the sheer number of repetitions and the amount of work that was involved, they then understood how my kids got so strong. It always amazed me that none of the coaches would accept the fact that basics make you strong.

In this day and age of instant gratification, where everything has to be quick, easy, and simple, we need to get back to basics and slow down to speed up. In other words, we need to stop shying away from and avoiding the struggle of mastering basic skills in order to reach our full potential. Take my word for it, you don't need to break your neck to realize that basics are the key to success in any endeavor in life.

31

GREATEST COMPLIMENT

As I mentioned before during my coaching career, I guided and coached numerous national champions. I had the great honor of being a USA National Team coach who traveled all around the world with the USA team. I was a master clinician at multiple national and international seminars, and the greatest compliment I ever received in my entire career came while I was grocery shopping. It had nothing to do with gymnastics and at the same time it had everything to do with gymnastics. To my utter surprise this compliment wasn't about one of my national level or elite gymnasts, it involved one of my entry level competitors.

One day, while strolling down the canned food isle, pushing my shiny silver shopping cart, I saw a familiar tan blonde woman pushing her cart toward me. It was Mrs. Engle, the mother of a former gymnast of mine. I looked up to meet her eyes and say hello, and as I did her face lit up like a neon sign.

She was grinning from ear to ear as she said, "Hi Gary so good to see you." Without even stopping to take a breath, she proceeded to tell me what her amazing daughter, Tori, was up to. She was talking ninety miles a minute in a high-pitched voice that made it almost impossible to keep up with all the accolades she was rattling off. To the best of my memory the conversation went something like, "Tori is in her second year at UCLA, she is the president of her sorority, getting straight 'A's in school, has a double major and is having the time of her life, and it's all because of what you taught her in gymnastics."

After I picked my jaw up off the floor, I honestly don't remember what I said back to her. I think I said, "All I did was provide an opportunity for your daughter to reach her full potential."

This is where I got a complete and comprehensive dissertation on what I actually did do. In a very matter of fact voice she told me how Tori had learned time management, goal setting, leadership skills, conflict resolution, and team building, which according to her was a direct reflection of my gymnastics training. Somehow, I don't remember writing all that down in my curriculum for my training program.

It wasn't until a few days later that it hit me like a ton of bricks that gymnastics was just a byproduct of what I was really teaching. It was one of those aha moments! My mind said, *Of course, in order to be a successful gymnast and more importantly a successful human being, you had to develop and master time management, goal setting, being a leader, conflict resolution, and be a great team member all at the same time.*

I thought the whole time I was just teaching good basic, progressive gymnastic techniques. But now I realized I was facilitating good basic, progressive life techniques. I had a whole new outlook on what I was really doing with my life, and all I could do was smile from ear to ear and light up like a neon sign too.

The thing that amazed me the most about my coaching career were all of the benefits my students got and how they incorporated those into their lives outside the gym. Gymnastics was the byproduct of what I was really teaching. It wasn't about the gold medals or all the team championships. It was about all the things that were blossoming behind the scenes, and the lessons they learned from their journey. It was about learning leadership, work ethic, team building, commitment, consistency, respect, communication, perseverance, integrity, handling adversity, and philanthropy. My students took what they learned inside the gym and applied it to their lives by excelling in school, perusing what they loved to do, becoming entrepreneurs, going into cutting edge research, and so much more.

You don't need to break your neck or spend years training for athletic competitions. You can take from my experience, add it to your own, and excel in whatever you apply yourself to. Remember, **anything is possible**!

CONTACT GARY BUCKMANN

My intention is that this book has inspired you and helps you connect the dots of your own life recognizing *that everything happens for you*. I hope you have been empowered and now know that 'you too, can do the so-called impossible' in whatever challenge you may be facing.

I'd love to connect with you, I invite you to reach out and follow me through my website GaryBuckmann.com.

Finally, I have a request. I'd truly appreciate it if you would write an honest review of this book to help spread the message that *anything is possible*.

Thank you in advance for your time and energy and for connecting the dots of your own life which makes our world a better place.

Gary Buckmann

ACKNOWLEDGMENTS

I have so many people to thank for helping me create and finish this book. Nothing in life is ever created without the support of others, especially something that makes a profound difference in your life and hopefully in the lives of others. Without the support mechanism of many amazing people, *Broken to Brilliant* would have never materialized. I want to thank the following people with all of my heart.

First and utmost I want to acknowledge my mom and dad who are no longer with us, for loving and guiding me their entire life. It was their love and support in my formative years that allowed me to heal myself and recover fully from my accident. Thank you both for being incredible parents and loving me.

I will always hold a huge sense of gratitude in my heart for my coach, mentor and friend, Mr. Jim Gault, who is also no longer with us. Thanks Coach, for recognizing my unseen talent as a teacher and for your genius tutelage to develop and expand that talent. Thank you for being such a great example of following your heart to do what you love. And especially, thank you for giving me the opportunity to discover what I loved to do.

I would like to recognize and give a humongous thanks to all of my college teammates, especially Robert Harden, Maurice Williams, Tim Niles, and Rick Feuerstein for nurturing me back to health. Without their compassion, patience, humor and support the broken me would have never been able to become brilliant.

I also want to send out a special thanks to Kasey Mathews my masterful, magical, writing coach and friend. Without your expert guidance of how to organize my stories, teaching me writing skills to make my stories come alive, and what to expect when publishing a book, my dream of becoming an author would have never materialized.

Every once in while an angel blesses us in our lives. I have been fortunate to meet a true angel in writing this book. My dear talent manager, content editor, and now friend Cristen Iris is the embodiment of excellence, grace, and humility. Thank you Cristen for believing in me and taking me under your wing. Your genius input created a flow to the book that I could have never imagined.

Stacey Smekofske is my humble, selfless, powerful, very devoted line editor, and publishing guru. I can't thank you enough Stacey for holding my hand throughout the entire process of publishing, and for guiding me through all the important little details required for a book to be published. Thank you for sharing all your genius, giving so much, and becoming a friend.

Tara Mayberry is an artistic genius that created the front and back cover of my book. She actually took a fifty-year old photo of me cropped it, added shading and coloring and brought it to life. Thank you for your creativity, care, concern and eye for detail in creating an amazing cover.

I would like to send out a heartfelt thanks to all the

students I taught during my career who adopted my program and made me, and the entire staff look good with all their hard work and dedication. Your supreme efforts year after year were the reason for all of our success. Thank you all for being such incredible human beings.

I would like to express a special thanks to all my staff members, who enhanced and made my program so effective by using their own gifts and talents. You helped thousands of students reach their full potential and made my job fun, enjoyable and super fulfilling.

A special acknowledgement goes out to my daughter Diana, her husband Andrew and my grandson Lucas, my stepson Nick, his wife Jessica and my grandsons Jackson and Bryce for always loving and supporting me in everything I do. To my sisters Gail and Carol who put up with me their entire life and still love me anyway.

And to my supportive adorable wife Victoria who taught me how to love myself through her love for me. You are the sole reason I was able to write *Broken to Brilliant*.

ABOUT GARY BUCKMANN

Gary Buckmann has been speaking and mentoring the gymnastics world both nationally and internationally since 1976. For 15 years, Gary ran a successful business while traveling the world as a USA National Team Coach. His gymnastic school produced State, Regional, and National Champions multiple times.

Gary was inducted into the Chico State University Athletic Hall of Fame and the College Park High School Athletic Hall of Fame. He has been motivating, inspiring, and training athletes to achieve champion success. Gary now helps business owners and people from all walks of life to achieve their full potential. He has spoken at conferences and symposiums worldwide.

Gary lives in Northern California with his wife, Victoria. He loves to rebuild bicycles, something he taught to his daughter and grandsons, and he rides his own rebuilt bike with his wife several days a week. Gary loves to dance and travel. He spends time in his backyard caring for his pool, lawns, and garden. And he is a huge Alabama football fan. To this day, Gary works out and can do 20 pull-ups and 50 push-ups at age 69.

facebook.com/gary.buckmann

linkedin.com/in/gary-buckmann-69466042